Fall Back

Dedication

This book is dedicated to the first love of my life that took his last breath March 2018. I will love you until I take my last breath.

Looking Back on Time

Looking back on time

Why did I give it to you?

You didn't deserve it

You didn't cherish it

So why did I give all my time to you

Through all the months I have seen you

I didn't get treated like I deserved

So, I'll take that time and put it away

Save it for another day

Cause someday I'll need it

Maybe for a rainy day

Why Did I Say I Love You?

Why did I say I love you?

Was it really true?

I think it was? Oh yes.

But you didn't love me too

I said those three words

And it never really got heard

But now you don't care

All you can do is stare

But in your touch I can feel it

The love that burns inside

I cautiously wait for you to say

That "you're all mine"

Time is wasted

And we are through

Now I'm heartbroken and don't know what to do

Promise me baby that you'll come through

I wait for you right now

But I won't wait forever

Cause someone will sweep me away

Someday or never

Please be clever

Cause it's now or never

I Know Someone That Likes Me

I know someone that like me

He won't make me cry

He will never cheat on me

He's just how I want him to be

He doesn't get too jealous

I like that in him

He knows that he's mine

I won't trade him for the world

I know he wouldn't trade me

He would never ignore me

Or push me to the side

I like him too

He knows this as a fact

A Graduation

A high school graduation is so emotional

You don't know whether to feel happy or sad

You want to feel happy for them because they completed a goal

But then you feel sad because they might be going
away

It opens a new chapter in your and their lives

You might not get to spend as much time with them as usual

It's just so different

It feels like a long summer break from school that won't ever end

We Are Leaving Each Other

We are leaving and going our separate ways

You are a graduated senior and I'm and upcoming sophomore

You're going off to college

I'm going to a more intellectual school

We are moving further away from each other

For the first time in a while

But this time is different

We may never get to see each other ever again

But we will always think of each other

I will always pray to see your smiling face

But no one can promise that day we will see each other except for God

So pray with me for we may see each other again

Jealousy

It's in me

I think it's a trait

I get so jealous when you talk to someone else

Whether it's a girl or a boy

I still get jealous

Maybe it's cause I'm spoiled

But when you ignore me I get mad

So tame my jealousy and treat me right

Because we can be together all day and night

A Wedding

It's a beautiful thing

Two people being joined together

Being with that person for the rest of your life

Sounds fun doesn't it

When my wedding comes around

I will be so happy

A Special Day

A special day

It's coming soon

It's the start of a new beginning

One that I won't mess up

When this day comes

I will be so happy

Someone Who Comforts Me

The person that comforts me

Is not anyone you would choose

He's very outspoken and honest

Some people say he's shy

But when you really know him he's not

He's fun to be around

And fun to just talk to

Every time I speak to him

It lifts my spirits and

It makes me feel good about myself

Being Appreciated

It's such a good feeling

Being appreciated for things

Some people ask for lots of things

And never say thank you

Sometimes it's hurtful

Not to be appreciated

But when somebody says thanks you

It means the world all the way around

Someone That Gives Me Inspiration

The person that gives me inspiration

We have just been reunited

He's an old friend of mine

That just moved away

He gives me hope each and everyday

That I will find that perfect one

He inspires me to think outside the box

But he doesn't even know it

We have open and honest conversations

And it's relieving to me

A real conversation with a person with a brain

It's good to be around people with sense for a while

I miss him so much but talk to him everyday

Having Something to Think About

Having something to think about is such a good thing

Most people think about nothing all day

Others just have so many things on their minds

That they just can't find one thing to think about

But when you have something on your mind

Just think it out even if it's

Love, money, or something else

Just have fun doing it

Some Kind of Love

I'm in love with somebody

But I don't know what kind:

Friendship, Relationship, or Family

It feels like real love that will last forever

But I don't want to diagnose it too quick

He hasn't said how he feels about me yet

But I will know very soon

The only thing that I told him was that he is liked by me

He just stated that he has known for a long time

So now we are friends and I'm waiting for more

I don't know what's running through his mind

I wish that I did

Maybe he thinks of me all the time

Maybe he doesn't

I know that I'm always thinking of him because he deserves my thoughts

I'm finding more out about him everyday

It's so much fun and I need a good time

He's the person that makes me feel good inside

He knows just what to say at all the right times

He talks to me all day and night

In all his spare time

During his breaks at work

Right after school

In his busy time

Or all during the night

I appreciate his attention through all times of the day
He means so much to me

No matter what day

Saw Someone

I saw a very special someone yesterday.

He is the one that comforts me.

He listens to all my problems, etc.

To see him was such a good feeling.

I hadn't seen him in months.

I needed a refresher.

Now I feel better about myself.

He made me feel so good.

Hugging him!

Him squeezing me so tight.

I felt so secure in his arms.

I wanted to stay there forever.

But he was with his mother.

I didn't want to be disrespectful.

I miss him already.

He looked so sexy in his blue collared shirt.

OMG! I think that I need to leave it at this!

Knowing His Mother

Knowing his mother is a good thing

I know her

She knows me

That makes me feel even better about that situation I love this person

Knowing his parents are great

I adore his mother

His father is a preacher

His mother does hair

They both have respectable trades

He wants to be a marine biologist

He's in school for that now

But knowing his folks is fun

Someone I Like but Can't Date

We have dated before

We had a bad break-up

He played a trick that I thought was the truth

Bout a girl on the side

I thought "that couldn't be true."

So I broke up with him anyways

He then became my stalker

I still have many feelings for him

I know he loves me the most

I wish we could get back together

But it's too many things that's holding me back the

most First, I think he's gotten on my mother's bad side

Second, I'm moving away

For the rest of my high school years

I don't know what I want to do

My life is so stressed

I don't know if I can take it

I think I should talk to my mom

But I don't know how that will go

But I guess we will find out soon

Being in a Relationship

Being in a relationship

It is so fulfilling

I love it so much

Being single is so boring

With a relationship anything can happen

Going on dates

Having fun 24/7

Kisses all the time

Feeling so new

Always feeling wanted

Never feeling ashamed

A relationship is a beautiful thang

The Perfect Bond

What happened?

When did you get so mean?

I thought we had the perfect relationship

I wish I could take whatever I did back

I didn't want this happen

We need to fix this

I want our perfect bond back

Ready to Move

I'm so ready to move

Everybody is becoming so mean

I hate it

When I'm at school I have no worries

I'm so happy there

No drama like now

I don't have to try and make people happy

I don't have to get fussed at about stupid stuff

I'm just so ready to go

I want to cry

I can't wait

When I get there I will throw a party

I don't know I'm just so happy

That I got accepted

Breaking a Heart

Breaking a heart is not an easy thing to do

They could cry

They could become angry

They could never speak to you again

It can make you feel so bad

But you had to do it

Before things advance too far

If you would have did it later on it would be worse

Things would be much harder

He has fell in love with you

Which is a bad thing to do unless…

I love you a lot back

Your family fell in love with me too

Which makes matters worse

I don't know if my family fell in love with you but…..

Ya'll met that's good enough

Meeting a New Family

It's like trying new food

Except a few things are different

Like for instance he can talk

But there are alike ways

They both can smell good, taste sweet, and look good

Everything changes for a while cause you have a new person in your life They can stay nearby or live far away

Either way they're just a phone call away

Doing All the Work

I do all the work

I get zero credit

Back to back I'm doing things

Most people don't even appreciate it

Like my bro, he never says thank you

And my mama asks me to do more stuff than a boss tells all the employees at Walmart

I get tired of it

I never get a break

Countdown 'til School

I'm counting down the days

I'm ready to go

I want to see my friends

Who love me for who I am

They are not prejudice

They're nice

I can't wait to see them

In Love with Someone I Can't Have

He's everything that I want

He's everything that I need

We talk everyday but for different things

He has a girlfriend

I have no one

It has been a while now since I've had someone

I have finally found someone to connect with

He's on every level with me equally

Spiritually, emotionally, and mentally

If we were not meant to be then no one is

He is so perfect and he doesn't even know it

He knows that I like him but we don't really acknowledge it

He has been hurt in the past

So have I

I want to heal his soul

We complete each other but…..

What more can I do?

I have confessed of my love

He's still in a relationship

I don't want to rush love

But love is overflowing in me

I love being with him

All times of the day

We have grown closer and are continuing to grow

I could be with him forever

But I have to be patient

I need to wait this out

Good things come to those who wait

Wanting You for Myself

I'm wanting you for myself

I don't want to share you at all

I want us to get together

I don't ever want us to break up

But right now you're taken

What can I do about that?

I can't be with you all of the time

But I wish I could

Every minute I think about you

Every minute I care

Sometime my love for you is overwhelming

But something will happen soon

What God wants to happen will happen

So I will wait patiently

Hopefully I won't have to wait too long

Waiting makes me stronger

I'm growing everyday

I miss you

I love you

Why won't you come my way?

I know that we are best friends

Always 'til the end

But maybe we can be more

Like something we could have done before

I Love You

Every time I tell you that I love you

You don't believe me

How can I get you to take me seriously?

I want you for myself Can I have

you?

Will you come to me?

"I don't want to turn the page"

You make me laugh

Not make me cry

<u>I Can't Help It</u>

I can't help that I love you

I can't help that I get jealous

I can't control what I do

I can only think about the good

When I'm with you

Maybe that's a good thing

Maybe that's a bad thing

But whichever one it is

I just can't help it

That's just how much I really and truly love you

A Bad Feeling

I know that you are supposed to be with this special someone

I already know who he is

But he doesn't want to be with me anymore

I love him with all my heart

But right now he just won't budge

It hurts to the core to know that we are not together

He said "Let's just be friends'

I say "I don't agree with that but I guess I have to'

It's hard to be around him and not be
in a relationship together Everything
seems weird now

I don't want to talk or look at him

I'm hurt, I'm scared, and I need some help

I can't do this alone

It's bothering me past a certain extent

I think that I am about to cry

But I don't want him to see my weakness

I have to stay strong

I have a lot of things to do

I can't let one thing/person put me down

It's burning inside like coal on fire

I'm getting heartburn, need to throw it up

I have to cry it out but not right now

Why don't I have a friend?

A shoulder to lean on

I Love You (2)

A love so deep,

That I couldn't even see.

It crept to the surface,

To take a peek.

And what did I see,

A person that I found,

That wants to give their love to me.

I cherish it so much,

They could not even know.

No matter how I act,

Deep down inside you're all I think about.

You are my soul,

You are my heart.

Baby I wish that I had,

Been with you from the start.

I have learned to be honest with you,

You are honest with me.

I cherish that in you.

Even though sometimes we go through stuff.

You always have my back.

Baby you are mine and I love it.

You poured your heart out to me.

I love you for that.

Boo, I need your love

I never knew love could be so

strong,

Until I met you.

No one has ever loved me so,

I never understood.

But now everything is clear.

And I know what I need and want.

I love you.

Still Not Over You

I thought that we were through for good

Then I got a surprise text

I was so shocked

I had spent months trying to get over you

When we started talking,

All of my feelings rushed back

Love, anger, jealousy

I was so shocked

We have went through so much together

But never will I get over you

I love you

I'm Looking for Love, but Love Doesn't Want Me

I talk to this person day by day

But nothing seems to come our way

I love him for who he is

And he won't change that for anything

Thoughts run through my mind

Thinking of him

But I never know what he's thinking

And he never really tells me

Especially if it's about me

He just sits back and look

It makes me feel weird

But it's that special kind of weird

The one that makes you laugh

He is always on the way to save my day

And I'm always on call to save his

We have had some ups and downs

But we made it through together

So will you, will you ---

Be my prince charming forever?

The One I Want

The one I want

He can be stubborn at times

He's always flippy floppy

One day he wants one thing

One day he wants another

But it's not really a problem to me

Unless it's between me and another girl

A chick trying to steal my spot

I think that's a definite not

But he seems like he likes her a lot

But I don't like her being on his jock

So I just sit back and watch

Wondering what's going to take place

It's iffy because you may never know

But it's one girl who might take your spot though

You toss and turn at night wondering what he's thinking

Because his actions though the day......

Were kind of odd and skeptical

I wonder if I could be his special one

And the one that he wants

Not just for one lifetime

For us

Forever and ever

Don't Get Smart with Me

If I ask you to do one thing

Don't get smart with me

Don't tell me what I need to do

Don't tell me what my mama need to be doing

You are not my mama so deal with it

You never will be You don't have

anything to say to me BYE!

Finally Telling Him That I Love Him

We have known each other for so many years

But I never had the guts to tell him the honest truth

One day he finally asked me that question

That I have been longing for forever

It was like a dream come true

A fairy tale really new

While in the moment I thought of a book

A book I always wanted to be about me

But I never thought I could have that scene

When the moment really came

I was mostly shocked

"Do you love me?" was the phrase I heard

I kept silent to think should I tell him or not

So I said "yes"; why shouldn't I take a chance

He asked me why I kept it to myself

I told him because he had a girl and that was that

But now I think that he is thinking it over

He takes me seriously and I like that about him

We always have a good time together

No matter what the case may be

If we get mad at each other

The grudge doesn't stick for long

I love him but I don't know if he's going to be mine

Never Being the Same Again

He says "I don't like you like I used too"

But I still do

Just because I mess up once

The relationship is over forever

I'm so emotionally hurt

And I don't know what to do

I thought we would be together forever but I guess not

So I guess I will just sit here and rot

Even Though

Even though he said "it will never be the same again"

I feel this surge of love through him

I speak to him on and off to see if there's a spark

But when I see a little it just fizzes away

Other people are trying to tell me what to do

But sorry I don't take advice

No one knows what I have been through but me

So I'm the deciding factor in this review

I love him for him no matter what

He doesn't love me back

But I really wish he would

If he could see though all the lies and gossip

We could be together again

I have mixed feelings a lot of the time

But this I know is true

I want you to be mine

So, will you boo?

A Sometime-y Friend

When we are in class with each other people it's different.

But when we are together it's grand.

Sometimes you want to be my friend.

But sometimes I want it to end.

You might want to act right.

If you don't want to lose a friend tonight.

Do you want to be my friend or not?

If so you should treat me the same all the time.

Losing You

I'm losing my best

friend.

What am I to do now?

Who am I to talk to?

Who will comfort me now?

Who will make my problems go away?

All because of a girl.

I told you how I felt about it.

Nothing changed except for that one day.

I thought you were the friend that would stick by my side.

Maybe not.

I'm so so trying to be nice.

But my body won't hold me from keeping this hold.

I feel as though I can't move on unless this is resolved.

I shed tears daily over this situation.

I try to hold back but they keep falling like dewdrops on a tree.

I want us to get past this but it might take a lot of time.

Every time I see you her..........

I instantly think "why?"

Do I always have to be the victim?

Why should I be ignored?

Why should I be put to the side because of this one thing?

Why be so selfish?

What about me?

Do you care how I really feel?

Or do you just pretend..........

Stuck on You

I try my best to stay over you

But when you say a certain thing….

I just fall in that trap all over again

If a song comes on that reminds me of you I began to cry

I still love you I can't deny that

Even though we are not together I can still feel a spark there

Like when we stare into each other's eyes like love birds

It's like being on a totally different planet with just you and me

Sometimes I feel I have moved on

But even though it has been all these months since we've been together

I still haven't had enough time to get over you

But no matter what anyone says we have the last say so

Therefore, the question appears:

"Are you going to walk out of that door?"

How?

How do you consider yourself my friend?

If you keep secrets from me?

If you judge me?

If you love to argue with me?

If we never have good times together?

If we always fuss?

If you don't share anything with me?

If we barely talk?

If we can't function in the same room?

If I ignore you?

If you always want your way?

If you argue with my morals?

If you argue with my religion?

If you question my sin?

Not a Friend

Friends don't keep secrets from each other

So why are you still talking to me

Friends don't hide things from each other

Why are you apart of my life?

We were supposed to be tight

Like white on rice

But now we are as far apart as Kobe and Glen Rice

So don't bother me and don't speak

You have nothing to say so I don't want to hear a peep

Still Wanting You

I still want you

I can't really understand why

I have all the reasons not to

Then I feel all the reason I want to

Maybe love is here;

Or maybe it's not

Either way I still want you

Even though we are not together I still get jealous

Cause I want you to myself

And I don't want you to want anyone else

I don't want you to go with her

Anywhere or to anything

I want you to be with me forever

Because I love you

You are always on my mind

124% of the time

Finally Getting Approval

She finally said "yes"

I'm so excited

It's like a new chapter in my life

The trust is back again

It's something that I cannot hide

My mom is so great and wonderful

I can't contain my happiness

Even though we can't talk all of the time we can still feel the love

I Like You but I Can't Tell You

I have liked you for some time now

It's been buried deep inside

You have dated one of my ex-friends

And I think you date the other

But from now into the future you may never truly know

Even though you may ask I will not speak

Unless you ask me out you will never know

I am tired of messing up my life by being honest

So from now on it's going to be "I prefer not to" tell you

I will from now on be secretive

No one needs to know anything

Physics

I once had to take an intro to physics class

It was challenging

What I really like

But it's stressful to brain and body

Chocolate Rain

sing to chocolate rain tune

(funny YouTube video from my youth*:
https://www.youtube.com/watch?v=WwTZ2xpQwpA)

Chocolate rain

Brought me so close to him and –nd -nd

Chocolate rain

I love him dearly but it ain't the same

Chocolate rain

Now he's in love and I can't complain

Chocolate rain

And we are now apart, and not the same

Chocolate rain

I like him but now I can feel the pain

Chocolate rain

The story's ending now and bye bye bye

Chocolate rain *I do not own the rights to this song, thought it would be a fun interactive poem

Poetry & Music

Music and poetry

Are like my vents

It's how I let go of my emotions

The best way to do it

No matter what

Without it I would die

Poetry lets out love

Music lets out anger and frustration

Poetry releases betrayal

Music releases regret

They help me feel better

More than you would ever know

It's my therapy

That I have to have daily

I love them

A Different World

When I'm around him

I feel as if I'm in a different world

A better world

A perfect world

People dread me talking of him

But I don't care

I have love for him

Can't say I'm in love

I feel that way though

His smile is so perfect

And so is his personality

I love to be around him

People say I'm madly in love with him

But I would never tell him

I love his company too much

I can't lose him as a friend

He's grown to be one of my best friends

I'm scared to be denied I don't think I

could take it

AGAIN!

Thought I Had You

I thought I had you

I thought you were my friend

I thought you wanted me

I guess not

But now you are with her

The one I don't like

I despise the relationship……

Even though you think it's a secret I saw you holding her hand

And my heart broke at that moment

Just like a glass window

My heart is fragile

Maybe you thought it wouldn't hurt me

But I guess you were wrong

Now I'm broken

And sitting all confused

I have to ignore this issue

Or else I will tear myself apart

I'll just pull my heart away from him

So we can be far apart

Unsure Feelings

I have known you for about a month

You are the shyest dude I know

But you are also the funniest

Every time you get online I smile

We talk for hours and don't look at the time fly by

I think you're cute

You think I am too

I guess that's a start for the future

I don't know how long this will last

I hope it lasts forever

Cause I'm really starting to have feelings for you

I'm trying not to fall in love
My heart is protected by many
I'm trying to change my life around....

Cause you never know what will happen

So many times I've had my heart broken before

I don't think I need even more to go

I have faith though that you won't break my heart

I'm going to try and keep you in my life forever

Tired of Being in 2nd Place

He's my friend most of the time But

he's better when she's not around

Maybe I'm just jealous?

And want to take up all his time

When he's mad at her

That's all we discuss

Then she plays with his mind

One day she's mad at him

He's falling under her spell

Sometimes I think he likes me

But other times just not

Me and him have had this discussion before

But nothing is clarified now

I'm trying to let my feeling go away

But they just won't budge

Every time I see him I can't help but smile

I try to be mad at him

It's just not possible

Someone who makes me smile no matter what

He could say the most random thing

And we would laugh forever

That's why I love to be around him

He always makes me feel worthy

Even though he's not mine

I love spending time with him

Even if I'm mad

But I'm tired of being in 2nd place

As soon as she calls you

You come running

So what am I going to do?

Stupid

I feel stupid

Because I fell into your trap

I'm still caught in your web

Trying to escape

But you have a tight hold on me

I want to cry

You don't deserve my

tears

Do you deserve my

time?

I'm trying to put this issue in the past

It can't be in the past if it's always in my head

I can't focus on anything

Just because of you

Tests every day and my mind is blank

Unless I'm thinking of you

Fading

We are fading away

As time flies by

We are forgetting

Or just not remembering

Life is moving by so fast

Everything is just go, go, go

What about just stopping to look

Take note of what's around you

Time

We need time

Never thought I would say it

But it is true

I want to tell you how I feel

But time won't permit the truth

You ask and ask

But I don't answer the question that's bothering me

I might get hurt

I think to myself

Or could I just be free

A Change Finally Came

This guy I have known

For some time now

He was an average guy when we met

We talked everyday on the bus

We sat by the window daily

And chatted the whole way home As

time progressed…..

He became very abusive

He showed off for everyone

They knew his strength was so mighty

One day he got in a fight

So everyone definitely knew then

We hooked up

It was like being with the king

It didn't last long

He said we broke up cause of something stupid

He wasn't trying to break up with me for real

The break up was supposed to be a joke

But I took it serious and broke it off

So after things went back to the same

He started back being nice again

One day on the bus I got a surprise kiss

It was the best gift ever

Because it wasn't expected

I stayed shocked for about a month

Then went back to the same thing again

We started talking on the phone every weekend 'til 6am

I know a lot of stuff about him

More than anyone else

Sometimes I think that's special

But sometimes I forget all about it

After that 1st kiss the bus was awkward

He started blowing kisses to me when other people weren't looking

That made me feel kind of good and bad

Good because he was blowing kisses at me

But he always joked a lot

So I didn't know whether to take it serious or not

I felt bad because he didn't blow me kisses in front of people

But I just hoped for the best all of the time

Because I like him so much

No matter what he did I always was positive

After I moved he wanted to see me often

He came to see me the day after Christmas

He kissed me again and told me "Merry Christmas"

I felt like an angel in heaven

We stopped talking for a while

One day I got a text from him and I was at home

He started being real sweet when I got back to school

He was calling me baby, boo, and lover

I felt special but I thought he was playing

Since he's so playful it's hard to tell

But I kept asking him why he was being so nice

He said he's always been nice to me

Even though he knows that's a lie

And we argue about it everyday

I didn't say anything this time

He's trying to treat me right this time

I'm going to see what's going to happen

I guess we will see,

won't we?!?

Hurt

All of a sudden a person changes their mind

They just ignore what they have always wanted

There is nothing I can do about it

So I won't even try

I just try an ignore the pain

But it's just not working

It's all I can think about

My heart is slowly breaking

I never should have let my guard down

Never let it down for anyone

People only want to hurt me

They don't care about the real me

They just want to play with my emotions

To finally make me crack in the end

I feel like I want to cry

But I can't show them my weakness

I have to stay strong

I have to work hard

To be torn down like this

I wonder what will happen when this day splits

Day/Night

Stuck

I'm stuck

In a world of misery

I'm stuck

In a world of pain

I'm stuck

In between love

Won't Give it Away

I refuse to give it to you

……..my heart I mean……

I don't want it to be broken

I can't take the pain anymore

Unless I'm loved unconditionally

And I know for a fact

I will keep my heart for myself

No games

No players

The pain is too strong

To know people don't care

But you have a heart

Emotionally Sick

Emotionally…..

I'm sick as a dog

I don't want to eat

I don't want to drink

I want to lay around and mope

Just lay around and think

Think of how many times I've been hurt

I try to put those things behind me

But it doesn't seem to work

Special One

Jesse Murray

Special one

The one in my heart

The one that I cherish

The one that I shed tears for

The one that I will miss

Dearly miss

The one that was special

The one that meant something

One person of love

That I loved and he loved back

Supportive friend

My special one

Making Progress

Step by step...

Day by day...

Hour by hour...

Minute by minute...

Second by second...

I'm making progress with you

Now Mine

Now mine to hug

Now mine to kiss

Now mine to own

You own me too

I'm just so happy

For you to be with me

Now mine...

Now mine...

I won't let go

Wanting to Have You

I see you in front of me everyday

The thought of me being with you

The thought of me being away from you

It makes me want to die

I want you now! I will want you then!

I will always want you

Mixed

I don't know what to do

Should I believe you?

Should I trust you?

Should I doubt you?

Love. Hate. Like. Despise.

I try to convince myself daily that I don't love you

But my heart tells me the opposite of my mind

I barely know how to be mad at you

But you know how to shut me out

I feel so distant from you mostly

But I want to be inside of that brick wall

Being your second shield when the 1st is broken

Protecting you from life's disappointments

I need love too

I wish I could get it from you

Maybe in time I can

But for now I'm just mixed

With You

With you by my side I'm in love

With you by my side sometimes I get jealous

With you by my side I feel unworthy

With you by my side I want so much more

With you by my side I feel defined

Spending Time with You

It makes me feel worthy

It makes me feel wanted by you

Our late night conversations turn into bonding

When I hug you I feel as if you're mine

Maybe you love me? Maybe you don't?

But spending time with you is worth a bunch

I think about you every day and night even if I'm with you

My mind seems to wonder off when you talk

You make my pain go away

You know when to do the right things

Just when I am about to walk away

I thought I couldn't take it anymore

But you made me want to stay

You make me happy and make me smile

But I hope all this is worth my while

Cause through it all

You're just not some person

But you're the person that I would go through it all for

In Love with You

I'm in love with you

Even though I tried not to be

It's all your fault

You're the reason I can't leave

We had the discussion of me ever divorcing you

But I know I could never make myself do it

We have been though a lot in the last 8 months

But it was all worth it

It made our relationship stronger

Feels like we could endure anything

When the time comes we have to be strong

And hide how we feel

Our love does powerful things

Often compared to "The Notebook"

I smile every time I see your face in my head

I think of all the good things you say

You make me happy I can't deny

It's also not good to lie

I know we will always have our ups and downs

Cause all relationships do

But unlike other relationships I know we'll make it through

Because I'm in love with you

My love is so strong

I would never let you go

Cause baby I'm in love with you

Trust Becoming Our Bond

From the beginning I thought it was all a game

But as time passes by I see that things have changed

We have fallen in love and that's no lie

We couldn't even stop it if we tried

But now my trust has finally turned over to you

I hope you don't break it cause I really am trusting you

Trusting you to do the things I always knew you could do.

A Love So Strong

A love so strong

To endure all the pain

A love so strong

To overpower anything

A love so strong

To make one's wishes come true

A love so strong

That the rules would just not do

To endure all things

And shame the rest away

To make the other one happy

For just one day

But one day is not enough to last this lifetime

The only thing to last as long as we both need

Is the thing that's in both of our hopes and dreams

The wonderful thing called marriage

The thing that could come soon

The thing that would always make me smile

By knowing I belong to you

The World That Lies Beneath

On the outside I'm fine

But the inside is all torn into shreds

It's like looking at a mirror & not knowing what's on the other side Emotions rise daily

Occurring with different situations

One minute you can be happy

And one minute feel like you have been shot into a million pieces

But you can't let the emotions overtake you

Cry only in darkness

No one should see your weakness

Crouched down in a dark corner

The tears are allowed to stream down

Cry as much as you want then

Letting all of the negative thoughts of the day leak away

Once you're all done smile

Think of the positives and carry on your day

Or end your night

But let no one know what lies beneath but you

Summer Days

While grasshoppers are hopping

The grass is growing

People are picnicking in the park

The sun is shining to make things grow

Kids are swimming

That's what happens on summer days

Different People

Writers love to write

Journalist have exciting jobs for writing newspapers

Teachers don't like when their best student leaves

Doctors enjoy helping people

What would we do without?

Counselors to give advice and listen to problems

Deserve

Do I…

Deserve your love?

Do you…

Deserve mine?

Do we…

Deserve each other?

Never thought I could be happy

But now I'm there

With you by my side

The Way You're Treated

It hurts me to know you're hurt

Continuously! Every Day!

When does it stop?

When does your pain go away?

When can I take you by the hand to tell you it's okay?

I want to save you

Away from this world of hurt and pain

But right now I'm incapable to help

It seems as if I make the problem worse

Maybe I should leave you alone

Maybe things will get better

But you say you need me

I say you don't

But again you say you need me to

survive So I'm here!

Holding your hand from miles away

I will support you and be your shoulder to cry on

I shed tears for you every day

To know that you're being hurt

I don't think you should be treated this way!

<u>Haven't Spoke in 6 Days</u>

I know that you're in a fix

I'm sorry about that too

But no calls for 6 days

I couldn't believe it to be true

You're leaving Tuesday

Without so much as a goodbye

I want to hear your voice

Before you board that plane ride

I'm starting to feel lonely

Without your companionship

I know you love me

But I need to hear it

Say you love me

So I can believe it's true

Not Being in Your Arms

Not being in your arms

I remember how cold the world is

Looking down upon everyone

Not being in your arms

Not able to cry freely

And have someone tell me it's alright

Not being in your arms

I have a silent plead to be

In your arms safe and sound is where I want and need to be

The Tears I Cry for You

Sometimes they're from sadness

Sometimes they're from missing you

Sometimes they're from madness

But mostly from missing you

Missing telling you how much I love you

And how much I really care

Thinking about how beautiful our arguments end

I couldn't have this with any other person

Cause any other person isn't you

I lay up each night and think of how empty my bed is

Then hold my bears tight and think of you

But usually it doesn't suffice

Seeing you in my dreams doesn't seem to help either

It only makes me want you

more So get to me faster

43 days to go! It feels like so long

But then when that year is over

Again I will be gone

But further away this time

Even though I'm not trying to

But these state lines are drifting to and fro

One day we will be reunited together for good

When that day comes there will still be tears

Tears of happiness and joy

And thoughts of us never separating

And everlasting joy

Our Heart

Our hearts grow together as one

Day by day being more entangled

Neither of us try to escape the change of stormy weather

Fights and smiles we share them all together

We were two but now are one

We breathe the same breaths

Our heartbeats are in sync

Our love is strong as the chains that hold us together

The foundation of our love is right

From the friendship level up to trust

Trust is developed over time

But I must say that's coming together as well

Our love is so strong I can feel it miles away

I breathe I love you at night

In response I hear her say 'Baby I love you too'

One tear drop falls every night

To remind her how much I care

As she's imprisoned in her house

I feel imprisoned in my mind

If one of us is imprisoned then we both are

We are one until death

Death is the only thing to keep us apart

Our Future Together

Our future

Will take place in the company of one another

Our love will surround our future

More fully than ever

Our wedding day filled with love and peace

The privilege of saying 'I Do' to you

Being yours forever

The thought makes me smile

Looking in your eyes I see your passion for me

The love you give me is unconditional

The love I pass to you is the same

Straight from my heart

I know you think I won't be faithful

But I would love to prove you wrong

I love you baby! Only you!

Healing You

I'd like to think I'm healing you

Because your past was so cruel

I want to make you forget it all

But it doesn't seem to move

You say my love makes it better

I hope for that to be true

Because baby, baby I want to heal you

Hurts Me

I know you're hurting

But it hurts me to

I know your past is killing you

But I'm trying to fix that too

I'm trying to get you to see

The world through my eyes

The wonder that I see in you

Even though our pain is different

Yours hurts me too

Undeserving

I'm undeserving of your love

You're too good for me

Baby you spoil me

What should you do with me?

I don't deserve your greatness and all you've given to me

But you constantly give me everything a girl could ever need

I love you baby

You're the best I ever could ask for

The girl of my dreams

The woman of my future

All that pleases me

Cold Tears

Tears fall down my cheeks

Notifying me of the feeling

Love. Madness. Sadness.

Thoughts of you carry the most

The tears that are the heaviest are for you

You tell me how much you love me

I cry because I can't believe I deserve you

Every day I wake up to think it's only a dream

To find out my dream is a reality

Happiness has found me

And happiness is happy with me

But still the tears fall for my love for you

My passion to keep you happy and going

Baby my cold hard tears are for your soul

Lonely

I'm lonely

But surrounded

People talking all around Nobody

wanting to listen

I'm the abnormal one

I'm in love with the female

My love story is not important

I can keep it to myself

It's not to be shared

Nobody in the family wants to hear it

I'm screaming inside and still no one listens

When I'm silent no one listens

I have my pen, paper, and phone

They will listen

They are not a part of my lonely

Fighting For Your Time

Always

I will be doing this thing

I don't like doing it

I wish it was automatically mine

But there's life

Life takes away my time

People. Jobs. School.

Take away my time

So again I will continue to fight

Because your time

It's worth my while

Making Her Happy

Making her happy

Well I'm trying

I do all I can

Still don't feel it's enough What's wrong with me?

Why can't I make this be?

I just want her to feel free with me

Every day it seems to get harder

I don't know what to do

I don't know what it takes

To truly make and keep her happy

Definition

People think when they find someone it's their other half

But you make up yourself

You have to be able to stand on your own

I see my special someone as my definition

She defines deeply into what I already am

She compliments me by standing by my side

The love of my life is my definition

Your Touch

Soft as feathers

Smooth as stone

Your touch follows me all day long

I yearn for you to hold me

I feel safer in your arms

You protect me from the world's lies

You're my guardian angel

Sometimes I can't believe it to be true

But your touch leads me on

Craving Your Love

A love so full

A love so true

I so faithfully want to be with you

To have and to hold

For all my days long

Your love conquers me

So I can never go too far

Craving your love

And all that comes with it

Never leave me

Cause I need to stay in it

Your LOVE

The Feelings I Have With You

I feel safe

I feel sound

You give me a complete sound mind

I might be mad

But you know what to do

Flash your smile

And I'll breakdown

Whatever it is I will carry you

I think of our love

And how limitless it is

The un-conditionality

The freedom of our kiss

Being with you is total bliss

The feelings I have

Don't really matter

As long as I'm with you

Nothing else matters

Pained

The thought of us breaking up

It constantly pains my heart

The stab of the knife that I wish not to feel

My love is too strong to break this ordeal

We fuss and fight

But that's not enough

Even though it still pains me sure enough

My love for you is above all pain

But between all of this my heart is still pained

Us

We are on edge

I need us in a safe place

You are my refuge What's

wrong with us?

What's wrong with me?

I need to fix this

To set things straight

To make you love me

To make you see

That I am the girl I was always meant to be

Fading Away

We are slowly fading away

Whether you see it or not

You're slowly losing me

Right there on the spot

You never seem to hit just the right button

Not a good thing because you always end up sucking

Making me angry every single day

I'm trying to be happy in every single way Yet

when I see you with her and your happy all the

time

Why can't you seem to shine while you're on my mind?

You steadily pout, groan, and moan

About every little pain in sight

Obviously I can't make you happy

You telling me this fact

So why stay with me when I'm ugly and I'm fat

I see no point for you to be with me

When you are so much happier with her

I hope one day you will realize

And act like you honestly know

<u>You and Her</u>

You and her

It pains me to see

That you and her are really meant to be

Ya'll laugh and fight

But are always happy Why want

me?

Your happiness is there

And so is your attention

So I'll just disappear And just

won't care

My Fears

I can't conquer them without your help

I can't fix it without your patience

If you can't stay with me

My heart will be broken

All of my fears would come true

If you cheat

I wouldn't know what to do

My heart would have been falling over you

My mind gone out of control

My stomach always in knots

My eyes playing tricks on me

My body telling jokes

My fears over taking me

Nothing left behind

<u>Reunited</u>

Back together

Feels so right

Everything was so wrong before

Goals back on track

What will happen next?

Not Wanting You

You don't entertain me anymore

I know everything about you

Our life has become boring

I don't want to be with you anymore

You rarely excite me

You take care of me

You treat me right (mostly)

I don't dream of you anymore

And I sometimes don't want you

So not wanting you

anymore Is that an option?

I hope it is.

I hope I can bare it.

How long will it tick on?

How long can it last?

There is no way to fix it

There is no way I can

Moving On

Moving on

To a different place

To start again

My education rate

My future coming

My past behind

The present is moving on

With a different piece of mind

Trying to start new

To keep my mind clear

But you're still here in my thoughts

Trying to get rid of you

But it's not happening

Wanting to live and breathe

With no worries

So moving on

Is it something I can do?

Moving on

This will be something new

Available for purchase on AMAZON

Please leave a review

Facebook: XBAlloway
Instagram: XBAlloway
Twitter: XBAlloway
Goodreads: XBAlloway